The Passive Income Blueprint:

Create Passive Income with
Ecommerce using Shopify, Amazon
FBA, Affiliate Marketing, Retail
Arbitrage, eBay and Social Media

By

Income Mastery

Table of Contents

How to Build an Online Empire from Scratch

Before we begin I have a free gift for you from Russell Brunson - for those of you that don't know Russell Brunson is, he's the man that created Click Funnels. In my opinion it's the best funnel website out there and it has also helped create the most millionaires. Any form of passive income you are going to build you will 100% need to leverage funnels of some sort. If you're reading this book, then you want to be the best in your industry. This book will give you the play by play to have people PAYING you for your advice. I am able to give you his best selling book for free right down here. I only have a few copies left so please get them while you can. Just click this http://bit.ly/giftfunnelbook

Introduction

Earning a living takes time, effort and a lot of work. But the problem with most jobs is that once you clock out, you're not earning money anymore. That's no way to get ahead, especially if you're wanting to take some time off now and then. However, more and more people are realizing that it is possible to make money while they sleep, with the power of Passive Income.

The internet has created a vast amount of opportunities for you to develop your very own Passive Income engine, a system in which you use different online services and tools to slowly generate wealth for you at all hours of the day. The internet never sleeps and with billions of people visiting websites each and every day, there has never been a better time to develop your own passive income stream.

The goal of this book is to help you, the reader, pick a few passive income ideas to work off of. We have 50 time-tested methods of generating money online for you to review. You don't have to do everything on this list, but if you picked three or four and worked diligently to set them up, you can be making money in no time!

What is Passive Income?

Passive Income can be defined simply as making money without actively contributing any work. While most jobs generate active income, where hours worked = hours paid, passive income relies instead on creating interesting or attractive products and then setting up a method for customers to find said product with minimal active effort on your part. By building a strong system that attracts people from the outside and converts them to buy whatever product or service you are offering, all you need to do is maintain what you have built, which takes minimal effort and time commitment.

However, it is important to note that building a passive engine system requires plenty of work before it is ready to go. This is not a get rich quick scheme, where you haphazardly set up a website and then watch the dollars roll in. Instead it takes discipline, hard work and a willingness to try over and over until you finally figure out what works best for you. Passive income is like firing a rocket into space. You want to put as much fuel as you can in the rocket at first, because taking off requires a ton of effort. However, once that rocket breaks through the atmosphere and is in zero gravity, pushing the rocket takes considerably less energy. Your work, time and dedication to building a passive income engine will determine the ultimate success of your project.

Generating Passive Income

If you want to generate passive income, then you will first need to invest either time, money or energy into a project. Depending on the results that you're looking for, you may need to invest large quantities of all three. While it may be easy to think that you can get rich online without much investment, the truth is that most big earners either invested a significant amount of either time or money into their work.

Passive income is a reflection of what you have invested. If you aren't willing to invest resources adequately, you won't see returns. There is simply no way around it. The good news is that while some types of passive income systems require a lot of money, others, such as the creative fields, can be done relatively cheap.

For those who are on a shoestring budget, you must be willing to make up for your lack of funds in effort. The harder you work on a project, the more hours you put in, the bigger chance you have of success. There is no guarantee that you will succeed for the first time, especially if you are working in a creative field that often requires some kind of a budget for advertising. However, hustle and elbow grease can go a long way in helping you to achieve your goals of passive income.

Creating an income goal

As you're preparing to embark on your passive income journey, it is important to determine what your goals are. Do you want to supplement your work income, adding a few hundred a month to your paycheck? Or are you wanting to go the full route and focus on replacing your entire paycheck with passive income? Neither goals are impossible, but the first one should be relatively simple, but the second option would have to be treated like a second job in terms of preparation and execution.

Your goals should be tempered with reality. You most likely won't be making thousands of dollars within the first few months of embarking on these projects. That isn't to say thousands can't be made, but if your expectation is too high, you may be tempted to give up when you aren't seeing the results that you want.

Instead, try to create a simple, attainable goal that you can reach within a few months. Then, once you've reached that goal, you can evaluate your methods, the time it took and then create realistic expectations for your next goal.

Create a business plan

Once you have figured out what kind of income that you want to be pulling in, you'll need to create a comprehensive business plan involving your chosen methods of generating passive income. This plan needs to include a timeframe, multiple stages for development and what you are expecting when you execute.

Part of the business plan is educating yourself in your chosen field. There are virtually unlimited sources of knowledge online, both paid and free that can greatly teach you the ins and out of the passive income system you want to develop. Don't waste your own time making mistakes that beginners make. Instead, take as much time as possible to educate yourself on the subjects, so much so that you could teach other people about how it works.

Prepare to Adapt

One thing to note too, when it comes to online income models is that the internet is a rapidly changing environment. Legal policies, popularity and trends can change in a moment's notice. You must work to stay as up to date as possible about the type of passive income system you are using.

Embracing the Success Mindset

Success is not an end state. It is not a final place that you arrive, kick off your shoes and then say "ahhhh, I'm finally there!" Because life is in a constant state of flux, you never know how long a project or passive income engine will stay profitable. What was popular today may end up wildly hated tomorrow. We simply don't know what the future looks like.

So, it is important to realize that success is not a destination, but rather a mindset. It is a mindset that requires a willingness to learn, a willingness to endure hardship and a willingness to try and try again. Failure is going to be the most constant thing that you face. There is simply no way around it. You are going to have investments that return nothing, projects that fall apart and unexpected disasters that get in the way.

Success is only possible when you overcome those failures, when you push through the disappointments and get back up on your feet. The success mindset requires you to realize that failure is a guarantee in the entrepreneurial world. But the good news is that failure isn't nearly as bad as it is cracked up to be.

If we look at success and failure as end states, we can quickly grow discouraged when we land in the failure category. We grow weary and may become convinced that since we have "failed" we cannot "succeed." And then, we fall into the trap of the failure mindset, the idea that something going amiss or wrong is the worst possible thing. The truth is, nothing you do as an entrepeneur will go right the first time.

The success mindset is nothing more than the ability to keep going, regardless of what happens. You must try, adapt and keep pushing forward. You'll find that no matter what endeavor you pursue, if you hold to the success mindset of never stopping, you will ultimately find financial reward in your projects. But if you hold to the traditional notions of success and failure as being end states, you will end up collapsing under the pain and sorrow of things going wrong. If entrepreneurship was easy, then everyone would be doing it.

Top 50 Online Businesses to Consider

#1: Amazon Kindle Direct Publishing (KDP)

Amazon Kindle allows for anyone to upload a book of their own making and then sell it online. Thanks to this option, traditional publishers can no longer prevent interesting books from reaching the market and touching the lives of fans.

If you're a creative who has always wanted to turn your writing into something profitable, then selling your book on KDP is the way to go. It's incredibly easy to get your book online. In fact, the hardest part will be the actual writing of the book.

Tips for Success

Write to Market

Selling books isn't the easiest of tasks, but fortunately there are ways to generate sales. By doing market research on what books are selling right now, looking for an area with low amounts of competition and high amounts of sales, you can start writing books purely for the purpose of selling to the market.

So, instead of writing a book and then trying to find people to sell to, you would learn what is popular and write a book in that genre. Writing to market helps to naturally generate sales upon release, as most readers are picking through the new release section to find interesting titles.

Get a good cover

While they may say that you can't judge a book by its cover, the opposite is true when it comes to marketing. A cool, eye-catching cover can be the difference between life and death for a book.

When doing market research, look at the top performing books in the genre you're writing for and get an idea of what people come to look for in covers. If there is one major investment you make in your book, the cover should be it. A great cover can get you plenty more sales.

Write a series

The best way to increase passive sales of a book is for it to be part of a series. That way, when a fan finishes the first book, they will naturally move to purchase the second one and third, so on and so forth. The longer the series, the more potential you have for sales across the board.

Frequently Asked Questions

Q: Is there a startup cost to using KDP?

A: No, there is no initial startup cost for using Kindle Direct Publishing. All you need is an Amazon account and then you will be free to put your book online, free of charge.

However, you can expect to spend money on things like book covers, hiring an editor for your book and advertising for the book once it has been released.

Myths about KDP

Myth: You have to be a big-name writer to make money

While it is true that those writers who have established followings are able to make money, the truth is that as long as you are willing to do genre research and write to market, you can make money too. Granted, you won't be making thousands per month, but you could quite comfortably make a few hundred a month if you are able to find the right combination of genre and market demand.

Myth: Once you release the book, the work is done

This is another myth that most unsuccessful writers believe. Writing the book might be the hardest part of getting it online, but once you have released the book you must spend time and energy on marketing. If you are creating a book series, then you must market it as much as possible, that way you can plant the seeds for more sales later on. If you're looking for a fire and forget type of passive income opportunity, KDP is not for you.

#2: Fulfillment by Amazon

Fulfillment by Amazon, or FBA is where you sell products online, but Amazon takes care of things, like shipping and handling. All you need to do is ship your products to an Amazon fulfillment warehouse, and they take care of the rest. This allows for you to sell products on Amazon, which is the biggest online store in the world, and not have to worry about keeping inventory in your own house.

FBA is a great way to make money if you're someone who likes to find cheap products in the real world, perhaps products that are on clearance or out of season, and then sell them online for more. One such application would be toy sales. Some toys are harder to find during holiday seasons. By purchasing them during the off-season and putting them up on Amazon during Christmas, you could potentially increase your sales.

FBA is perfect for those who enjoy acquiring products and then selling them online. This works best as a passive income system, as Amazon does the bulk of the work. Your job is to find the items, send them in and then create the descriptions online. After that, it's just a matter of customers who are searching to find your products and buy them.

Tips for Success

Create a Private Label

If you're looking to establish repeat business from customers, then you might want to consider creating what is known as a private label.

A private label is essentially a brand that you create, putting your label on generic products so that customers will come to know your brand. So when they get an order in, they won't just be getting a few items from a random company, but rather from "XYZ Brand." Private labels work great for generic products that have no brand themselves. To create a private label, all you'd need to do is find a generic item that you want to sell, find a steady source of those items, such as from a manufacturer on Alibaba.com, and then create a logo and label to apply to those products. This will create a brand identity for your FBA business and hopefully generate repeat sales from those who come to trust your brand.

Look for Suppliers

The biggest challenge you will face when using FBA is finding a supplier. Everyone has a different method. Some prefer to go out on weekends, hitting garage sales and clearance aisles, looking for quality goods that are cheap but can be sold for a profit. Others prefer to find some unique products and negotiating with the supplier. Finding a supplier who will sell to you for cheap and in bulk will help prevent any lapses in inventory, which in turn translates to more sales. So, if you've found a good niche product that is selling, you may want to consider finding a supplier who can steadily provide you with orders.

Write Good Descriptions

Part of selling means that you'll need to pitch the product. However, when it comes to Amazon, most of the time the customers have landed on your product because they are looking to buy something relevant. A good, accurate description of the product, giving clear specifications about what the customer is getting will help to move them to convert. False claims, exaggerations or vague descriptions could end with you having to issue out refunds, and those hurt your bottom line!

Frequently Asked Questions

Q: What is the cost of Fulfillment By Amazon

A: There are two costs primarily associated with FBA. The first is shipping. Once you have acquired the products that you want to sell on Amazon, you'll need to actually ship them out to the Fulfillment Center. These shipping costs come out of your own pocket and can vary based on how much you are sending and the size of the packages.

The second cost are the fees that Amazon charges for using their service. Since Amazon handles all of the shipping, handling, returns and other customer service issues, they will charge you a fee per product sale. This fee is based on a scale, taking into account the size of the items you are selling. The second fee is for shelf space. While your products are in the FBA warehouses, you will be required to pay a monthly fee for how much inventory space you are taking up.

Fortunately, these fees are not terribly big and as long as you are pragmatic with your planning, shouldn't cut too deeply into your bottom line.

Q: Can I sell anything with FBA?

A: No. Amazon is unlike eBay, in that they have strict quality control standards. If Amazon is going to be selling products, even products they don't own, they want to ensure that their standards of quality are met. This means that certain products and product types are banned from being sold. With their standards changing from time to time, it would be best to check with FBA's home page first to see what products you are allowed to sell using their service.

Myths about Fulfillment by Amazon

Myth: This is just like eBay

When eBay first hit popularity, just about everyone started looking at all their old junk as a way to make money. Some even were able to make a living, finding vintage items that sold well and putting them up for auction, only to watch people greedily outbid each other. However, FBA is not about single sales. Rather, FBA is about steadily selling a large volume of products to customers. If you have a signed baseball, use eBay, but if you have ambitions to run your own online store and sell volumes, us FBA.

Myth: Market saturation means I shouldn't waste my time

Let's face it, even as you're reading this, Amazon is growing larger and larger. They are a huge company and with FBA, there is quite a bit of competition out there, all vying to sell their wares. This market saturation might make you worried that you will be lost in a crowd of other products, unable to sell anything because a single search brings up over 9,000 results.

However, making money on FBA simply requires that you find a niche market. Amazon is not a mall, but rather it is a search engine. People use Amazon to find products that they want. Your job should be to first figure out what underserved market exists on Amazon and then capitalize on it. Finding the niche market pretty much guarantees sales. Of course, finding a niche takes a lot of time and research, but once you find that perfect area to market, you will get a lot more sales. Don't try to run with the competition, instead break away and find an area that isn't being served well.

#3: Start a Blog

A blog is a great way to generate passive income because blogs generate web traffic. Nothing is more valuable than getting attention, especially in this modern online era, where there are a million other things trying to capture a user's attention.

By creating a blog, you will be able to direct people toward the various products that you are selling, sell adspace or even affiliate market. All you need is a good theme, a good subject and plenty of great content.

Tips for Success

Blog about what you love

If you are going to have a successful blog, then you're going to need to pick topics that you genuinely are passionate about. Sure, certain types of blogs might look successful from the outside, but often times the only reason they are successful is because the writer is passionate about the subject. So write about what you love, whatever topic it may be. Sure, in the end you'll want to generate income from your hard work, but you should also love what you write.

People are looking for authenticity when it comes to things like blogging and can quickly tell when the writer is being insincere. If you're only blogging just to make a buck, that will be picked up quickly and you won't have much of an audience. So, even though you may want to use your blog as a vehicle for generating passive income, you must still be willing to put in the time and effort to win the trust and admiration of your audience.

Focus on Good Content

Above all else, a good blog needs good content. Before you begin working on monetization, you'll need an audience who is dedicated and loyal to you. The only way to get that audience is by creating content that is interesting, engaging and entertaining. It doesn't matter what field you have chosen to write in, you will want to ensure that each post that you make is of good quality.

Blog Every Day

When you're just starting out, the biggest weakness that you will have is lack of content. When someone lands on your website, they will have the opportunity to explore and see what interests them. If you only have two or three posts up, they most likely won't stick around or continue to follow you. This can be remedied by choosing to create new blog posts every single day. This will be an exhausting task at first, but until you have a sizable backlog, you'll need to just put in the hours.

Once you have enough posts to where it would take a person more than an hour to read through, you can begin to ease off the gas and focus on creating a healthy blogging schedule that will work for you. Some post once or twice a week, others pick a set number of days, such as Monday/Wednesday/Friday to update. Regardless, the more consistent you can be with your releases, the more stable traffic you will generate over the weeks.

Find a blogging network

Networking is extremely important when it comes to blogging. Having friends who are able to direct their own traffic over to your website will help you out, especially when you're first beginning. Blogging networks aren't hard to find, you just need to spend time time searching for networks that are in your target demographic. Then, reach out to the people in charge and see what it would take to join their network. Some networks are open and friendly, others require to have a certain level of popularity first.

Guest Blog

Another great way to increase the number of people visiting your blog is to invite another blogger to write on your blog. This will take that blogger's viewers and transfer them over to your blog for a short time. Hopefully, a portion of those viewers will start looking at your own content and begin to follow you. Likewise, you can also offer to write a guest post for another blogger in a similar field to you. This will help create backlinks that can then be followed to your website.

Frequently Asked Questions

Q: How does blogging make money? Aren't blogs free?

A: A blog itself creates attention from viewers. This attention can then translate into free, targeted marketing for other products that you have. For example, if you have a book series, and you blog frequently, the people who read your blog will be constantly pitched to buy your books. This is strong, targeted marketing that can keep converting, well after you've stopped actively marketing for a product.

Another method would be to simply sell ad space on the blog. With a sufficient number of viewers and the proper ads being pitched to viewers, you can generate income simply from people clicking on banners. Other ways of making money through blogs include:

- Being paid by companies to create "sponsored posts" '

- Having a donation system, such as Patreon, to turn followers into financial supporters
- Using affiliate links when talking about products.
-

Q: Does my blog theme matter?

A: It depends. While blog content management systems out there like WordPress allow for a huge variety of themes, you may wonder how much a blog theme matters. Truthfully, as long as the color scheme of the theme isn't offensive, as long as people are able to navigate intuitively, you shouldn't worry too much about the theme. After all, people are visiting your blog in the hopes of gaining valuable information about whatever subject you cover. Don't worry about dazzling them with your web design. Most people will settle for a dark blog theme with revelant content than some expensive theme with only two blog posts on it.

Myths about Blogging

Myth: No one reads blogs anymore

While it is true that visual content has grown quite a bit thanks to YouTube, the idea that no one reads blogs anymore is patently false. In fact, the opposite is true! As more and more people have come to trust online sources of information, that means they are also spending more time reading blog posts. In fact, according to Hubspot, companies that publish 16+ blog posts per month get nearly 3.5 times more traffic than companies that only publish a few blog posts! Those numbers clearly indicate that if anything, people are still extremely interested in reading blog posts.

Myth: You have to be a brilliant writer to blog

If you're not naturally a writer, you might feel exceptionally awkward when it comes to creating content on your own. However, people in this day and age aren't looking for beautiful, flowery prose or long, elegant sentences. They are looking for information, for something of value. As long as you are able to write in complete sentences and keep typos to a minimum, people will often focus more on what the content has to offer more than your technical writing skill. So don't be uncomfortable when you first start out writing, you'll get better over time. As long as you are able to get your ideas across, you should have no trouble with blogging.

#4 Flip Domain Names

If there is one resource out there that is rather limited these days, it would be domain names. Every business out there needs to have a domain. However, domains are bought and sold by domain registrants like GoDaddy.

One curious way to generate passive income would be to engage in domain flipping. This is a bit like prospecting. You simply purchase a domain name when it's cheap and then sit on it until someone who has quite a bit of money comes along and offers to buy it from you. Then, you make the sale and enjoy the profits!

Domain flipping is a risky business, but the overhead is extremely low. Most domains cost only around ten or fifteen dollars, meaning that for a few hundred dollars, you could hold a wide variety of domains that could sell for much more than that.

Tips for Success

Research Domains that sell

Before you drop any money down on domains, you should spend time doing research, so that you can develop the necessary ability to identify which domain could make you money. Of course, in the end there really is no way to tell exactly which domain names will sell well, but by doing research on past behaviors, you can try to predict what the future will be.

Buy Domains cheap

Don't waste your money on domains that are too expensive. There's no reason to go any higher than what the current market rate for a standard domain is.

Sure, you might think dropping a few thousand on a single domain could net you results later on, but at the same time, you have no guarantee that anyone will want to buy those domains later on. So, save money and focus on bulk instead of one or two big ticket domain names.

Buy expired domains

By using a domain registry lookup, you can find which domains have recently expired and then snap them up. This practice can be quite lucrative, especially if the individual or company who let the domain lapse wants it back.

Frequently Asked Questions

Q: Is domain flipping legal?

A: Absolutely. Just because an individual or company has a copyright or trademark to a specific brand or phrase doesn't entitle them to the online domain name. You are perfectly within your rights to purchase any domain name on the market and if someone wants it, they will have to pay you for the right to use it.

Q: Is Domain Flipping a guaranteed thing?

A: No. There is no way of knowing that the domain you grab a hold of will be worth anything in the future. Sure, you may get lucky and snag a domain name that a company will want later on, but this is more akin to speculating on the future. Still, in terms of investment, it can be tremendously profitable compared to most other types of investments.

Myths about Domain Flipping

Myth: Domain Flipping is unethical

This is false. Everyone has the same access to domains, built on a first come, first serve basis. This is no different than purchasing real estate, only for a company to then make an offer to buy the land from you because it's necessary for their growth and development. You wouldn't fault someone from buying good land and then flipping it, nor should you fault anyone for buying a domain and selling it for a profit later on.

#5: Sell Online Using Shopify

If you have products or services that you'd like to sell from your own website, then you might want to consider setting up a Shopify site. Shopify is a web host that is specifically designed for e-commerce, with helpful plugins and systems that will allow for you to make the most out of your web space. Best of all, Shopify handles most of the heavy lifting for you, it allows you to track traffic, evaluate sales, create coupons and even automate aspects of the shipping label process!

Tips for Success

Add Review Plugins ASAP

Once you have your Shopify website up and running, you will want to have a review plugin set up as quickly as you can. This will allow for customers to leave behind good reviews for your products, which in turn will influence other people to make purchases. Reviews are one of the most essential parts of selling a product online. The first thing a potential customer looks when evaluating your product is reviews, to see if what you are selling is a good product. If you don't have reviews available at a glance, such as with a star rating system, you will be denying the customer the ability to properly evaluate your product, which can cause hesitation in them. And hesitation may lead them away from making the purchase right there!

Have Good SEO

Search Engine Optimization, or SEO, is what will make or break your Shopify site. SEO is essentially when you use keywords that people are frequently searching for online. By utilizing the right keywords on your website, you can increase the chances of your site coming up when people search on engines such as Google.

SEO is extremely important for generating organic traffic. While targeted marketing goes a long way, it is often quite costly and takes a bit of time to master. SEO, on the other hand, can be cheap once you invest in the proper tools that allow you to learn what keywords are most frequently being searched for. Then, by placing relevant keywords on your Shopify site, you will be able to gain a search engine presence. This means that when people begin to search for those keywords online, your website will end up as one of the results. The more relevant your product is to their search, the higher you will appear on the search results ranking.

If you're going to be successful with using Shopify to create passive income, then learning how to utilize SEO for the best is an absolute must. Fortunately, there are plenty of free resources online that teach how to use SEO to get the most out of your business.

Create Good Visuals

Selling online is a visual art. Good product displays and attractive images can work wonders in enticing visitors into making the final purchase. Likewise, bad visual design can cause people to click away from your site, losing out on the potential for sale.

If you want to have a successful Shopify site, you'll need to invest some time and money into having both good visual design for the shop as well as good visual design for images of the products.

Fortunately, Shopify does have plenty of themes to choose from. These themes are well made and take care of the heavy lifting of web design. However, for product images, you'll most likely need to invest in a good photographer to get the proper pictures that can really make the products pop.

Install the Right Apps

Shopify has the ability to add apps to your store. There are both paid and free apps. These allow for even greater forms of customization for your shop, improving customer experiences and even for generating more leads after a sale has been completed. There is no shortage to the number of apps that exist on Shopify.

So, once you have your website up and running, spend some time poking around the app store and adding as much as you can to improve the quality of your store.

Frequently Asked Questions

Q: How much does Shopify Cost?

A: Shopify offers several different levels of service, where they offer a flat, monthly fee to use their platform, as well as a surcharge on every purchase made using a credit card. These different levels offer different features, but the lowest level is fairly cheap, when considering that you are getting a great web host and a ton of features that allow for you to focus solely on making sales.

Myths about Shopify

Myth: Shopify is just another content management system, like WordPress.

While it might be easy to look at Shopify as a simple web host, the truth is that they offer all the tools you need to run your store. For a single, flat fee a month, you will have everything necessary to sell products. With Shopify taking care of just about everything, you will be freed up to spend time focusing on what actually matters: developing a marketing plan. You won't need to waste too much time creating a website from scratch and putting in each system, like with WordPress. Shopify already has everything you need.

#6 Employ a Virtual Assistant

One of the hardest parts about generating passive income is the fact that plenty of these projects require a certain level of maintenance. Very few of these ideas can just be created and then thrown out online. They require time and effort if you want to use the projects to make money. However, you might not have the time necessary to maintain these engines, or perhaps you want to find a way to limit your involvement even more, so that you truly are making passive income.

A virtual assistant is one of the best aids in your quest to develop a passive income engine. With the help of a virtual assistant, you'll be able to outsource the more cumbersome tasks of specific projects, such as handling your businesses' social media presence, or taking care of inventory issues.

Of course, this is one major downside with a virtual assistant, and that is the fact that they cost money to hire. You'll often need to pay an hourly rate to employ their services, however, the money they will be able to save you in the long-term, by handling customer service problems, running your social media or doing research can certainly be worth it.

Tips for Success

Use Freelancers

In today's digital economy, freelancers have become extremely valuable for filling in skill gaps. If you want to run a blog for your business, but don't have the writing skills or the time, you can instead simply hire a freelance writer to make some blog articles for you. Likewise, if you want to have good web design, but don't have the skillset, an online contract can make a real difference.

Have clear goals established

Your money is valuable and when you are using a virtual assistant, you'll want to save as much money as possible by reducing the amount of time they work. The best way you can save this time is by having clear goals established for them, so that they know exactly what you want. This will allow for them to go about their business effectively and quickly.

Frequently Asked Questions

Q: How do I find a Virtual Assistant?

A: The best way to find a VA is to either use a freelance website, such as Upwork, where you can create contracts and find freelancers, or to use a Virtual Assistant firm. Firms tend to be more expensive, however, you often get a higher quality of assistant.

Q: Can I trust a virtual assistant with important data?

A: Trust is a very important part of the work relationship with Virtual Assistants, however that trust does not come quickly. Rather than just hire someone out of the blue and give them all your passwords, you should work to establish a working relationship first. On top of that, by using a firm or a platform that provides freelancers ratings, you should be able to hire VAs with established track records.

Myths about Virtual Assistants

Myth: Virtual Assistants are too expensive

While they might appear to be costly at first, you have to do a cost-benefit analysis before you are able to determine if they are too expensive. If you don't have a lot of time to work on specific aspects of your business, you may end up suffering financially. Rather than limit your sales to try to save a buck, you can expand your business opportunities immensely by hiring a virtual assistant to take care of the areas that are either time consuming or beyond your skill range. You'll find that in the end, a good VA can generate much more than you are paying them for.

#7: Get into Affiliate Marketing

Affiliate marketing is a tremendous way to monetize a website that has a steady source of traffic. Affiliate marketing companies offer "bounties" in exchange for conversions that have been provided by your links. For example, if you were part of an affiliate marketing program for a pressure cooker company and you have a link to a pressure cooker on your website, you would get compensation if a purchase was made with that link.

Of all the different ways to set up a passive income engine, Affiliate Marketing is one of the most tried and true methods. If you are disciplined and work hard to put together a good affiliate marketing system in place, you could generate quite a bit of income.

Tips for Success

Focus on a Good Niche

If you want to make money through affiliate marketing, you're going to need to attract the ideal customer to your website. This means you'll need to identify a good niche and then stick to it. Some people make the mistake of trying to appeal to too many areas at once, but this only dilutes your audience. It's better to stick to one core niche in order to attract traffic that will follow your affiliate links than it is to have a larger number of people who simply won't convert.

Find the Right Affiliate Network

You'll need an affiliate network if you're just getting started with affiliate marketing. A network is the go-between, handling the deals between the actual affiliate company that is paying the bounty and the marketer, who will be advertising on their behalf. A good affiliate network will give you options of what product you will be marketing as well as assist with the actual mechanics of getting paid. You don't always need to work with a network to be an affiliate marketer, some companies or publishers offer their own programs, such as Amazon's affiliates.

However, an affiliate network can make a big difference in someone just starting out.

Be Transparent

One of the most important parts of affiliate marketing is being upfront when sharing affiliate links. Giving just a small disclaimer at the bottom of your articles mentioning that the links you are sharing are affiliate links and you'll be receiving compensation for any purchases made will help establish trust with those who visit your website as well as comply with certain communication laws that have gotten stricter about stealth marketing.

Frequently Asked Questions

Q: Are there any fees associated with Affiliate Marketing?

A: In general, no there are not. Affiliate marketing is a marketing service, provided to publishers and companies that are looking to promote their companies. They are the ones who should be paying you.

If you find a network or program that requires a fee, or some kind of financial contribution to get started, you should avoid that network. Those kinds of programs are either scams or unnecessary to get started with affiliate marketing.

Q: Is Affiliate Marketing Dead?

A: Occasionally, people may look at affiliate marketing, which is one of the older forms of making money online and conclude that the practice is outdated. This couldn't be further from the truth. The fact is, people are making more money than ever with affiliate marketing. The wide reach of the internet combined with the transformation of the marketing landscape has made things such as referral marketing and endorsements much more potent. Affiliate marketing isn't dead and plenty of people are making money.

Myths About Affiliate Marketing

Myth: I don't need to care about the products I'm pitching.

Affiliate marketing is built around the idea of trust. When you have people visiting your website and they follow your blogs, they are placing their trust in you. They are trusting that you won't steer them wrong with the products that you are recommending. If you pitch products that you don't care about, haven't verified or can't guarantee are actually good products, you could be potentially misleading your fanbase. Sure, you might make some money in the short term, but over time this strategy will cause resentment and may lose you on the opportunity to make even more money in the long term.

Myth: High traffic equals higher affiliate profits

Web traffic is extremely valuable. If you have a website bringing in ten thousand people a month, you might be excited to see those ten thousand people convert straight to being customers, swelling up your affiliate paychecks. However, the truth is that while traffic is good, it doesn't guarantee direct conversions. You should focus on finding good products that would appeal to the majority of your audience, while tempering your expectations. Usually, only a small percentage of any group will actually convert. This doesn't mean that your affiliate marketing efforts are failing, it just simply means that getting people to purchase things online can be difficult. Affiliate marketing is a great way to build passive income and high traffic can definitely increase the chances of making money, but don't expect your entire audience to convert.

#8 Start Dropshipping

Dropshipping is where you sell products without ever having to physically handle them. Thanks to access to big manufacturers online, using the internet to find them, you can create a storefront, sell products and then send the orders to the manufacturers to be fulfilled. This allows for you to sell products without having to invest the major capital usually required in running a business.

Dropshipping is one of the more successful online business models out there and thanks to websites like Shopify, which allow for easy integration, you can quickly build your own dropship websites selling niche products that will generate you money while you sleep!

Tips for Success

Find a great supplier

Since you don't have an actual inventory, you'll need to find a supplier who is willing to work with you on fulfilling orders. This will be one of the bigger challenges of dropshipping, as it takes time, energy and plenty of research. However, once you are able to find a great supplier, one who is willing to fulfill product orders. This requires usually a personal

48

connection with the supplier, so that they know you are legitimately running a business. Some suppliers might not even be interested in working with a business that makes only small orders, so be prepared to spend most of your time looking for ones that are willing to work with smaller companies.

Focus on offering cheap products

While dropshipping can be lucrative, the margins tend to be smaller, especially now that many people are beginning to take up the online practice. A great way to get ahead of the competition is to offer cheaper products. Most of the time, people are paying for brand names and can get the same quality of product from a generic retailer. By taking advantage of this, you could potentially create a stronger flow of customers by offering lower prices. However, make sure that you are still offering quality with what you are selling. You don't want people growing frustrated with your business model and switching to another competitor.

Try to get exclusive distribution

There is nothing that will help increase your profit margins than having an exclusive distribution deal with a supplier. Of course, for extremely well known products, this will be very expensive to negotiate, however if you aim for smaller suppliers, who have niche products, you could potentially land yourself an exclusive. This will limit competition and provide you with a higher rate of sales, since people who are interested in the products will have to go through your store in order to obtain what they want.

Frequently Asked Questions about Dropshipping

Q: Do I have to pay a supplier?

A: No! Most wholesalers are looking for avenues to sell their product and get paid when you sell the products for them. They make their money through this system. However, there are some shady websites out there, who will try to charge you for the privilege of selling their products. These websites aren't actually suppliers, but rather have contacts with suppliers themselves. They charge you and then turn around and simply submit your orders to the actual supplier. In other words, they are the middleman to a middleman. Never pay for the privilege of using a supplier.

Myth: Once a website has been built and a supplier found, the sales will come pouring in.

Unfortunately this is not the case. Remember, if you can dropship, then just about anyone else can. While the task of finding a supplier, building a good sales website are vital, you'll need to dedicate a decent portion of your time actually marketing what you are selling. This will require all sorts of different targeted marketing techniques, such as Facebook marketing. The good news is that most of marketing can be automated or handled by a virtual assistant, which means once you have done the heavy lifting of finding a supplier, you will be on the course for smooth sailing.

#9 Create and Sell Online Courses

If you have an expertise in a specific field, then you can turn that expertise into money! How? By simply creating and selling online courses that instruct individuals about your expertise. With a small investment of time and money, you can create a course series that can be sold to thousands of people online!

Tips for Success

Find your Passion

Expertise usually stems out of passion. If you are able to find what you are passionate about, you won't have much trouble with sharing that passion with others through an online course.

Build a lesson plan

A good lesson plan takes the learner through the basics, leading them to the intermediary topics and then finally, onto the advanced subjects. You should spend time working to develop the course so that it moves the learner at a steady pace through all three levels. Don't overload them with too much information at the beginning, or else they may grow overwhelmed.

Be entertaining

Nothing is worse than taking an online course that sounds like the person who is narrating is legally dead. Even if you aren't much of an entertainer, try to be lively, speak with enthusiasm and excitement. Avoid monotone and deadpan forms of delivery, as this can quickly kill a learner's own excitement about taking your classes.

Create a series

Online courses should be sold in batches, with multiple courses being part of a main series. Each course should be full of relevant and valuable information, but you should break it up into multiples so that you can sell customers a package deal. And, if a customer sees a single course that interests them, they won't have to pay for the whole cost of the package deal to gain access to it.

Frequently Asked Questions and Answers

Q: I'm not an entertainer, but I have a good course idea, should I pursue it?

A: If you aren't a good entertainer, are camera shy or have trouble reading scripts, you may want to consider hiring someone to teach the videos for you. They should be versed in the subject and capable of going off script, but should also be willing to stick closely to what you want them to teach. If you don't have the funds available for that project, then consider just practicing until you feel comfortable enough to record the videos yourself.

Myth: I have to be an expert videographer to make a good course

People aren't downloading courses for pretty looking videos or long, sweeping shots of landscape. They are downloading courses because there is something that they want to learn. While you should generally make an effort to ensure that your videos have some decent quality and are watchable, don't worry about getting fancy. People just want the information that you have for them.

#10 Develop an app

Apps are a great way to generate passive income, especially if you are able to develop an app that meets a market need. However, the downside to creating apps is that they take quite a bit of time and can be costly, especially if you are working on making something that requires graphic design. Still, once an app is in an app store, it will continue to bring in revenue to you for as long as it remains relevant.

Tips for Success

Be Unique

App stores are often full of a handful of really successful apps and then dozens, if not hundreds of clones and cheap imitations. While there is something to be said about trying to rush into a market with an app that is similar to what is popular, most of these efforts are weak and lazy. Worse yet, some apps even try to create the image that they are sequels to other, more successful apps.

If you want your app to be successful, you'll need for it to stand on its own. Work to create an app that has its own identity, an app that solves a problem that isn't being focused on in the current app market. It may be easier to just copy another idea that has been done, but unless you are able to do it better, what's the point? Why would anyone play a poorly made Tetris clone when there is already an official Tetris app?

Of course, this doesn't mean you can't improve other app models. You might see that certain app types all follow one formula and that formula is inefficient. Creating your own and releasing it, making it better than the original can be a great way to get rapid popularity. Still, this requires a commitment to doing something different than just the status quo.

Create incentives to share

Word of mouth marketing is extremely valuable when it comes to apps. A brand new app needs to make it to the top download charts as quickly as possible. The faster that an app charts, the more sales you can make. One of the best ways to ensure that your app is shared from customer to customer is to create an incentive for users to share. This incentive can be as simple as a referral code which gives both the user and the new person a benefit.

Be Kind in your Microtransactions

Creating an app that has microtransactions is one of the most standard business models that is accepted by most users. There is nothing inherently wrong with having microtransactions in your app, however, you must take care not to abuse the customer. You may find that it is easy and tempting to create a powerful paywall that prevents customers from using the best services, or in the case of games, have access to the best characters. However, this can create a negative image among fans and they may take the reviews to protest your microtransaction systems. Be generous in giving content and use microtransactions as a way to enhance the lives of customers, while still keeping things fair across the board.

#11: Offer Online Consulting

If you're looking for a way to make a large amount of money in a short amount of time, you might want to consider online consulting. While consulting is a way to generate active income, you could use that money to then finance other areas.

Tips for Success

Create a consulting identity

Everyone has an expertise in something, so you'll need a bit more than just knowledge in order to succeed as a consultant. You'll need to work to create a brand identity, so that people who visit your website will get a clear idea of what expertise that you can offer them. Sharp branding, a good website and testimonial will help give potential clients the idea that you can provide them with invaluable advice.

Have a good portfolio

A good portfolio is a necessity if you are going to motivate clients to look to you for assistance. This portfolio must be 100% honest about your achievements, which means you'll need to be accomplished in your field before you can consult. The portfolio should include professional work that you have done, relevant testimonials from former clients (if you have any) as well as links to the professional credits that you have assisted. This will help give your client the understanding that you are legitimate in your field. Trust is hard to come by, especially online, so by working on your portfolio and making sure that everything is above board, you can work to gain the trust of viewers.

Offer a free consultation

A free consultation, perhaps a free hour of talking can work wonders in customer acquisition. First off, it allows for you to interact with the potential customer and see what their needs are. You can learn what they are looking for and in turn, help point them in the right direction. Best of all, you'll be able to determine if this client is serious enough to work with. Plenty of consultants have to deal with clients who hop on, have huge expectations and only $100 to work with. With free consultations, you might be saving yourself a big headache.

Offer a referral bounty

Once you have your consultation business put together, you'll need to bring in clients. One good way to do so would be to have a referral program, where you offer a financial reward to those who refer work to you. So if you have a few friends who are active in relevant businesses, you can offer to pay them a few bucks in exchange for the people that they send their way. This referral program will help get your business going and more importantly, will help turn converted clients into recruits for you, as you'll be able to offer the referral bonus to them as well.

#12: Get into Online Auctioning

While selling through Amazon can be profitable, don't forget that online auction sites are still a thing! People still use eBay as well as other websites like Auctionzip to find valuables that can be hard to find. If you like collecting rarer items and selling them for a profit, then you should consider using an auction site to sell your products. After all, while Amazon is a powerhouse, they have strong restrictions on what can be sold. eBay, on the other hand, is peer to peer, meaning people know they are directly dealing with you, not some big corporation.

Tips for Success

Learn to identify valuable items

People who visit online auction sites are looking for either one of two things. They are either looking for an item that they can purchase below market value, due to wear and tear or aging, or they are looking for items that are hard to find in the normal online market. If you want to sell to the secondary market, you'll need to learn how to identify what items are valuable in the niche you are targeting. For example, if you decide that you want to start selling baseball cards on eBay, you'll need to spend time researching what cards sell for. Most importantly, you'll also need to determine the price point that most people are willing to meet in order to gain the product. This means that if market research indicates a baseball card will sell for $50 total, but customers are only willing to pay $30 for it, then you should start the bidding at $30. It's better to have a sale than it is to have something sitting on the shelf forever.

Offer Competitive Shipping

Most people are turned off by shipping prices. It's a strange phenomenon, but people dislike losing something more than they enjoy gaining something. The idea of paying money on shipping is often perceived as a loss and can discourage sales. However, if you work to provide free shipping and simply roll the cost of shipping into the cost of the product, people will actually be willing to pay more for the product. If you aren't able to do that, perhaps the cost of shipping would cause the product pricing to lose its competitive edge, try to do everything possible to lower the cost of your shipping. You don't want customers walking away from a deal simply because they don't like the shipping rates you are charging.

Have Good Photos

You might not be a professional photographer, but thanks to the way phones are being made now, you don't have to be. There is no excuse for having poorly lit, shoddy photos, especially if you are trying to sell your products. Pictures are how your customers will make the decision to purchase your product, so the more that you have, the better. On top of that, the easier it is for potential customers to view all sides and aspects of your product, the more they will be able to determine if the condition of the product is worth purchasing.

Frequently Asked Questions

Q: Which is better, auctioning or Amazon?

A: This is an age old question. Really, it depends on how you want to go about selling. If you want a single price point, one that doesn't move up or down, then use Amazon. However, if you want to sell an item that has the potential for increasing in cost, then an online auction site is the way to go. Sometimes a bidding war can happen between two buyers and that will be quite wonderful for you, as it drives the prices way up.

Myths about Online Auctioning

Myth: There's too much competition to use online auction sites anymore

While it is true that more people than ever are using auction sites, don't forget, auctions are about the *product*, not the competition. If you are selling rare and valuable things, antiques and collectibles, chances are you won't have a crazy amount of competition. While it is true that anyone can set up an auction online, they all don't have access to the same products that you do. This creates a form of scarcity that protects you from the sheer amount of competition out there. As long as you are selling in a somewhat unique field, targeting a niche market, you should be able to make your own way selling stuff on auction sites.

#13: Invest in Cryptocurrency

Cryptocurrencies, such as bitcoin, have made quite the headlines lately, with the spike in people investing, causing the price of Bitcoin to shoot upwards. Some people who were casual investors a few years ago even found themselves making hundreds of thousands of dollars when the prices skyrocketed.

Cryptocurrency investing isn't the easiest thing to navigate and it is risky, but if you are looking for an alternative to traditional investing, cryptocurrency is the way to go.

Tips for Success

Don't Chase Successful Currencies

While Bitcoin is the biggest example of success, there are plenty of other cryptocurrencies out there. In fact, new cryptocurrencies are also being created regularly as well. What you don't want to do is chase after a currency once it begins to bubble. For example, Bitcoin made headlines when it began to reach it's all time high of $20,000 a coin. And, like all bubbles, it dropped significantly in the following months after that high. Why? Because there were plenty of investors who were interested in realizing their gains, among a dozen other reasons investors sought to sell the currency off.

If you see a currency taking off hard, you might consider throwing your money at it, in the hopes of riding the wave to victory. However, this generally does little other than give an already successful investor an exit point. Instead of trying to jump on the coattails of winners, it would be better to focus on investing in the smaller currencies, or waiting for the bubble to pop and then buying when the currency you want is cheaper.

You Are a Trader, Not an Enthusiast

Cryptocurrency has no physical value in the world. It is purely a digital coin, created through a system that creates scarcity which in turn, makes it limited. While many say that crypto is doomed to fail because it has no backing in the real world, that's not really the point of trading. Trading is done so that you can make a profit, not because you're a fan of a type of currency.

This means that you should have an exit strategy prepared. When you buy into the cryptocurrency, have both an acceptable price point that you are targeting as well as the minimum loss that you will accept before you sell off. Don't just invest in crypto and hope for the best. This can lead to disaster. Instead, make sure that you have a clear exit strategy. Don't assume that a spiraling currency will get better and certainly don't assume that a sudden spike in value will keep its upward momentum. Like all trading, you need to buy when it is low and sell when it is high. Determine which level of profit you want and then hold to that.

Be Prepared to Lose What You Invest

This is a harsh truth, but crypto is an unwieldy beast. With the lack of regulation and oversight, combined with the strange whims of the internet, cryptocurrencies can do really well or really poorly. Some might never take off and others may end up making you rich. But you should never invest any money that you aren't ready to say goodbye to. Never invest with money that you will someday need and certainly don't use your life savings on the project. Instead, take money that you are 100% willing to never see again and use that as your investment. This will help temper your emotions when it comes to trading, which will then help you think straight.

Frequently Asked Questions

Q: How many cryptocurrencies are there?

A: Too many! Since anyone can develop a cryptocurrency system, new currencies are being created all the time. Some of these currencies are made as jokes by online jokesters but others are used as part of a serious endeavor. You should exhibit discernment when evaluating a new cryptocurrency to invest in, to determine if there will be any interest in that currency on the wider market or if this currency was just created as part of a fad.

Myths About Investing in Cryptocurrencies

Myth: Since Crypto has no real world value

This is a common myth that is perpetrated by those who are from the traditional financial world. While it is true that you can't hold a Bitcoin in your hand, there are some vendors out there who accept Bitcoin as a payment option. And as the years go by, slowly, some vendors are beginning to accept that there is financial value behind cryptocurrencies and accept them as payment for goods or services.

Myth: Hackers can easily steal my cryptocurrency

This is another myth that is often spread by the media. You're always reading some news story about how a hacker managed to steal a few million dollars' worth of Bitcoins. However, with the way that cryptocurrency is designed, the only way someone can access your money is if they have the actual unique code to those specific coins. And since you, and you alone, hold that unique code, you can't be directly hacked unless you share that code with someone else. Most of the time, these cases of "hacking" are really situations where cryptoinvestors used a fraudulent bank that offered to hold cryptocurrencies for them. Then, when the bank had access to enough of these codes, they simply transferred the coins to themselves and absconded with the money. This is as much hacking as someone borrowing your debit card and then buying a boat online is. So as long as you are discerning with who you share your code with, if anyone, your investments will be safe.

#14: Get into Commodities Trading

While cryptocurrency is one wild, wild west of an investing situation, it is not the only way to make passive income through investment. One, significantly more stable method would be to get involved with commodities trading. Thanks to online access, you can become a commodities trader in the comfort of your own home, buying and selling trade goods with the click of a button.

Tips for Success

Get Seriously Educated

Commodities trading is no small task. It is a serious business that has been going on for thousands of years. If you want to make money through trading, you'll need to take your education on the matter very seriously. Spend time studying, take a few online courses and get prepared as much as possible for this endeavor. After you've put in the proper time, you should be ready to get started for real, but don't just jump in half-cocked. Treat your education in the matter as the most important part of making money.

Frequently Asked Questions and Answers

Q: How Risky is Commodities Trading?

A: All forms of investment contain risk, that much is certain. However, one advantage that commodities trading has over other forms of trading, such as the stock market, is that commodities are actual raw goods and materials that demand exists for. This means that while prices can go up and down, depending on real world events, there will always be a basic demand for these products, which limits how badly they can drop down. So while there is always some level of risk associated with any trading, commodities trading is less risky than others.

Q: How much do I need to get started?

A: Commodities trading does have a higher entry point in terms of price. In general, most brokers require a decent amount of money to get started, usually between the $5,000 to $10,000 range. These larger sums of money, however, do allow for you to create a steady stream of income with trading. Anything lower usually makes it harder to turn a decent profit.

Myths about Commodities Trading

Myth: You have to store the commodities

While it is true that you are purchasing commodities online, you are actually just purchasing futures, which means you aren't actually responsible for the storage of said commodities. SO if you've bought futures in wheat, you won't have to accept a large shipment of wheat, normally because you close the contract before the product delivery notice is sent. Only large businesses store and house commodities, the small investor doesn't have to.

#15: Create Video Content for YouTube

Thanks to YouTubes' monetization system, the more people that watch a video, the more money comes rolling in for that video's creator. If you're someone who has a creative streak and wants to generate passive income, then creating videos on YouTube can be a great option!

Tips for Success

Be Different

Since anyone can create a YouTube channel, it means that there will always be a large wave of people who all have similar ideas. Some YouTubers may even model their own personalities or content stylings after other, more successful Tubers. However, the problem with this style of thinking is that most of these junior league YouTubers aren't very good and as such, creates a gigantic pool of mediocre content for viewers to wade through.

Instead of trying to follow after the crowd, differentiate yourself. Try to figure out what unique style you want to present to the world and then develop that. It's no good to waste your time and energy on being exactly the same as everyone else. Instead, you should give it your all to stand apart.

This should give you the benefit of helping other people see that you aren't an imitation of those who are already successful, and increases the chances of them following you.

Make a lot of videos

Frequent video updates are important for YouTube viewers. Some YouTubers manage to create videos every other day, and some are crazy enough to release daily videos. That might be a little too much for you at the beginning, but you should still be dedicated to creating a large amount of content that can be released over the weeks. Aiming for at least one video a week is a good starting point, but you should create a few videos in bulk, to give yourself space so that you can make a few more videos without there being any lapses in upload scheduling

Frequently Asked Questions and Answers

Q: Is there any cost to making YouTube Videos?

A: For uploading videos on YouTube, not at all. It's a free service that anyone can use. However, there are usually costs that go into productions and those costs can vary, depending on the quality that you are aiming for. However, if you're looking to make just a simple, informative series of videos, you can probably pull it off for free.

Myths about Making Money on YouTube

Myth: I just need to wait for a video to be discovered and then I'll be swimming in cash!

The myth of discovery is one of the more pervasive myths in the creative world. While it is true that there is a chance of something going viral and generating a significant number of viewers and, as such, income from ads, those chances are insanely low. You shouldn't build a strategy hinged on the idea of a video of yours suddenly taking off. Instead, focus on learning the fundamentals of good video design and keep a strict release schedule to build a staircase leading up to success.

#16: Become A Social Media Influencer

If you enjoy using social media websites like Facebook or Instagram, then you can actually work to develop a voice as an influencer.

Influencers have the power to influence the way their followers make purchasing decisions and lately, companies have begun to recognize that value. As such, there are networks that are willing to connect Social Media Influencers with businesses. This can turn your passion and hobby for Social Media into dollars and cents!

Tips for Success

Be Authentic

More than anything, people are looking for those that they are able to trust. By being honest, upfront and authentic with your followers, you will demonstrate that you are trustworthy. Remember, people can generally sense when you are being authentic or not. If you want to build yourself up as an influencer, you have to earn trust and the only way to get that is by being honest about your positions, your business relationships and your current feelings.

Be Active

Becoming a social media influencer isn't a casual affair. You can't just post once or twice a week and hope that will be enough. Instead, you need to eat, live and breath social media. Post as much as you can, engage with people, ask questions and comment on other posts. In order words, be as active as possible. This is really the best way to steadily build a following while also staying deeply engaged with those who are interested in you.

Frequently Asked Questions and Answers

Q: Is there a method to becoming an Influencer?

A: Yes! There are plenty of different approaches you can take to becoming an influencer, however, they are all bound together by one common thread: dedication. The pathway to becoming a social media influencer is not an easy one and it is not for the casual participant. So, while you can develop and follow specific methods offered by other guides online, it's important to remember that there is no magic bullet. Becoming an influencer primarily takes time and hard work.

Myths about Social Media Influencers

Myth: Paying for followers can help me grow

While it may look alluring, the idea that all you have to do is open your wallet and a bunch of followers will arrive, the truth is far less appealing. When you pay for followers, hiring some company online that promises that you'll get X amount of followers for X amount of dollars, you are most likely violating the social media platform's terms of services. In addition, these followers are just bots, fake accounts that won't actually interact with you. Sure, they may swell up your numbers temporarily, but your account could possibly be flagged and they will be culled after a while, leaving you with nothing.

#17: Earn Royalties from Photographs

Companies and individuals often need great photographs for their projects. Rather than spend the money on hiring their own photographers and going through the trouble to get a good shot, they would prefer to simply pay to purchase a photograph online, through companies that offer stock art for a price.

If you're a photographer, with a keen eye and a great sense of style, you can turn your hobby into money, by submitting your photos to stock art galleries. There, customers can browse your pictures and offer to purchase them, paying you a royalty for their use.

Tips for Success

Use a stock photo sales site

There are plenty of websites online that offer stock photos for licensing. If you're just starting out, you may want to simply sell through them, contacting them and showing them a good portfolio. If everything goes well, you'll be able to put your own photos online and get a royalty when they are purchased.

Create your own sales site

If you don't want to share the profits, or feel that your portfolio is strong enough to warrant selling stock images on your own, then you should build a website and offer the pictures that you want to sell.

This will take more marketing energy and time, but on the other hand, will increase your profit margins as well as build specific relationships with customers. This can translate to more sales later on.

Frequently Asked Questions and Answers

Q: Do I lose my copyright when I sell stock photos?

A: No! Most stock art is licensed out to a business, for either a specific time period or for a specific product. So you don't have to worry about losing the copyright to your photo. And sometimes, there are options for a company to purchase the rights to the image itself, able to use it royalty free. This option, however, can be very costly for the company which means you'll make even more money!

Myths about Selling Stock Photos

Myth: There's no way to get noticed in today's overcrowded art world

While it may be easy to feel this way, especially when you consider the sheer number of premium services that sell stock art, the fact is, thanks to online connectivity, it is very possible for you to become noticed. With the advent of social media sites like Instagram, which allow you to post pictures of your work, you could easily find willing customers who have a direct connection to you. If you're worried about visibility, then you just simply need to focus on getting creative in how you share your products with the world.

#18 Invest in Real Estate Investment Trusts

Real Estate Investment Trusts, or REITs for short, are types of real estate investments that are publicly traded on major stock exchanges. This means that if you are the type who is interested in investing in real estate, but wants to hedge the level of risk required, you could instead choose to invest in a REIT, which work similarly to stock portfolios. Of course, instead of investing in a company, you're investing in real estate properties.

Tips for Success

Invest in a REIT ETF

Since REITs function similarly to other types of stocks, that means you can mitigate risks even further by investing in exchange-traded funds. These ETFs are collections of different REIT portfolios that offer annual yields. This is a great, safe way to invest in real estate without taking on in any of the risks involved with directly purchasing land.

Pay attention to market conditions

While REITs are less risky than straight up purchasing real estate, this doesn't mean that they don't carry any risk. Property values are highly contingent on economic factors and market conditions. This means that a REIT can potentially increase or decrease in value based on what is currently happening in the market economy. Pay attention to market conditions when deciding which type of REIT you want to invest in. If you think we're heading towards a downturn, then you might want to shy away from purchasing REITs that are based on retail locations.

Frequently Asked Questions and Answers

Q: How do I make money off a REIT?

A: REITs are legally required to pay out 90% of their profits as a dividend to their shareholders. Since real estate property generates income through rent, this means that the money must be divided amongst those who own stock in the REIT. Most of the time, 100% of the dividends are paid out. These dividends are exempt from taxation, which translates to higher dividend payouts as well.

Myths about Real Estate Investment Trusts

Myth: REIT investing is the same as real estate investing

This is incorrect. Real estate investing requires an entirely different set of skills and evaluation abilities than investing in REITs. Why is this? Because real estate is a physical product that you will own, whereas a REIT is simply another type of investment for you to add to your portfolio. This means that REIT investing is more similar to trading stocks or investing in ETFs than buying real estate.

#19: Become a Silent Partner of a Business

If you have a large amount of capital and want to put it to work, without doing much work yourself, then you might want to consider simply becoming a silent partner to a business. A silent partner is just that – silent! They don't have any input on the business side of things, instead of allowing for the capital that they provide to work for them.

Tips for Success

Believe in the Company

Becoming a silent partner is risky in the sense that if the business fails, you will lose your entire investment. With that in mind, you must have a high level of faith not only in the company but in the people who are running the company as well. You must be able to trust that without your directions or oversight, that they will be able to operate the company in a way that will generate profit. This isn't easy, and your search will undoubtedly be long. However, when you finally find a company and a business owner that you believe in, it will certainly be worth it!

Join an angel investor network

An angel investor is someone who simply is willing to provide capital to a business or idea without requiring a personal connection. If you wish to become an angel investor, you can join networks where individuals and companies provide pitches, in the hopes of being able to raise funds for their businesses. This can allow for you to have a perfect outlet to become a silent partner, as all you need to do is provide the funds and let them get to work.

Frequently Asked Questions and Answers

Q: How do I make money by being a silent partner?

A: When you provide capital to the company, you gain equity, which will rise in value depending on the success of the business. So if you provide equity to a small company that ends up growing, you are entitled to a portion of those profits they make. Furthermore, you can always sell your share of the company, which will then sell for much higher than what you have invested.

Q: How do I find businesses to partner with?

A: The easiest way is to look around offline, at family and friends to see if anyone is currently working on a business venture. If that doesn't work, you might want to consider investing online through angel networks, although working with strangers can be riskier and there are no guarantees that you will get a return on your investment, so you'll have to trust them fully before you get started.

Myths about Being a Silent Partner

Myth: You have to be rich to invest

Truth be told, not every company needs hundreds of thousands of dollars. Some small businesses, especially savvy startups may only need a few thousand to get started. You don't have to be insanely wealthy to invest, you just need to find a business that would derive extreme value from your own level of wealth.

#20: Rent Out Your Space Using Airbnb

If you have property that you aren't using, or a spare bedroom that isn't doing much right now, you can rent out your space using Airbnb. Airbnb essentially allows for people to turn their own properties into little hotels, connecting vacationers with property owners. This is a great way to generate passive income and turn unused property into money.

Tips for Success

Check the Rules First

While Airbnb can be quite lucrative, especially if you have a unique or spacious property, you must make sure to check the laws of your lease as well as local laws. Some residential areas are not zoned for commercial use and by using Airbnb, you could be potentially risking a lawsuit from your landlord or even from the city. Don't throw all of your profits away by illegally renting out with Airbnb. Instead, work to make sure that everything you are doing is on the level.

Create a good guest experience

You really don't need to do much when it comes to being a good Airbnb host. In order to create a good guest experience, you just need to make sure that the rooms are clean, the rules of the property are clearly stated and that certain things like toiletries are stock up. Some hosts even go so far as creating gift baskets to greet their guests when they arrive. The harder that you work to provide an excellent guest experience for them, the better chances that you get a good review. And remember, when it comes to online booking, reviews are some of the most important things that you can have. Good reviews equal more bookings! And more bookings equal more money in your pocket!

Frequently Asked Questions and Answers

Q: What happens if a guest causes damage to my property?

A: Perhaps one of the biggest worries about letting strangers into your property for a weekend is the fear that something might get damaged. Thankfully, Airbnb offers something known as the Host Guarantee. If damages are higher than the security deposit, they will cover up to a million dollars worth of damage. This guarantee does have certain limits, however, so you should check with their official policy to get a better idea of what is covered.

Myths about Airbnb

Myth: Guests will be destructive to my property!

While there are certainly instances of guests being disrespectful to property, the fact of the matter is that 99 percent of people who use Airbnb are perfectly behaved. This is for two reasons, the first being that most people don't want to cause problems for others. IF left alone, they will behave reasonably and not cause any damage. The second reason is that most guests don't want to lose their security deposit as well as their privileges of using Airbnb. A bad guest can end up being blacklisted from the website, which means they won't be able to go anymore to enjoyable, unique locations for their vacations. They'll just get stuck with visiting regular, boring hotels.

#21: Get into Lending Club Investing

If you have a bunch of money sitting in your bank account and it's not really going anywhere, you might want to consider investing with the Lending Club. The Lending Club offers investors the ability to invest their money into different loans, that will be borrowed and then paid back by the borrower over the period of a few years. This is a great way to get higher returns than just letting your money sit around in a low-yield savings accounts.

Of course, as with all investments, lending does carry risks. The return rates are based on the riskiness of the borrower. So you can get high yield returns by loaning money to high risk individuals. Or you can keep the risk lower and get lower returns. It's really up to you about how much you are willing to risk in order to get returns.

Tips for Success

Start Slow

Lending with websites such as the lending club can be exciting and it is possible to overextend yourself, if you invest too much money at once. Instead of going full steam, try to start out slow, investing only a small sum at a time, to get a feel for how the system works. This will help you determine if you want to continue investing with peer to peer lending sites or not.

Build a portfolio

The Lending Club itself allows you to split up your investments into smaller "notes" these notes are then combined with other investments which make up the entire loan. This allows you to mitigate risk even further, by investing only a small amount of money into high risk loans, if you so choose. Of course, the more notes that you own, the greater your returns are.

With that in mind, you can work to build a portfolio of many different notes, which will allow you to build up the ideal returns that you are looking for. If you're looking for aggressive, high returns, you can invest primarily in notes that are high yield.

If you're wanting a more moderate approach, seeking to balance risk and yield, you can create a mix of high and low yield notes to even each other out.

Frequently Asked Questions and Answers

Q: How much do I need to get started with The Lending Club?

A: In order to open up an account with the Lending Club, you'll need a minimum deposit of $1,000. After that, you can then invest in as small as $25 notes, which will make up your portfolio.

Q: Is peer to peer lending for everyone?

A: If you're risk averse, hate the idea of losing money and just want to play it safe, then you should avoid peer to peer lending companies like the Lending Club. However, if you are comfortable with the idea of losing out on an investment, then peer to peer lending can be another great tool in your toolbox!

#22: Credit Card Cash Back Rewards

Imagine that every single time that you spend money, you also made money. That would be pretty great, wouldn't it? Well, thanks to the power of cash back rewards from credit cards, making money while spending is possible! All you need to do is enroll in a credit card program that provides a cashback option. Depending on your credit score, you can qualify for all sorts of different types of rewards, ranging from getting a flat percentage back when you spend, to even getting airline miles!

Tips for Success

Transition Your Spending to Cashback Cards

The best way to make full use out of cashback cards would be to transition all possible spending to your credit cards. This allows for you to get cashback on all your monthly spending, your bills, etc. However, there are some caveats here. The biggest is that you make sure to pay your credit card bill in full on time, every time. Credit card companies use these rewards as motivations to use their services, but remember, they make their money through generating interest. By paying off the card in full every month, you are ensuring that you won't have to pay any interest. On top of that, you get the bonus of free money coming in!

Frequently Asked Questions and Answers

Q: How can I get a good reward card?

A: The best way to get a credit card with a reward system is to shop around and look for the ones that would suit your lifestyle the best. Some offer cashback only on gas, while others offer flat rates. The most important part about these reward cards is that the top tiers are offered to those who have exceptional credit, so you might not always qualify for the best of the best.

Myths about Credit Card Rewards

Myth: Applying for Cards Hurt Your Credit Score

This is one of the most common myths out there. While certain type of applications do appear on your credit score, credit card applications are known as "soft" hits, which mean they don't hurt your credit score unless you are applying for new cards non-stop. If that's the case, you very well could end up hurting your credit score.

Myth: Credit cards are just a bad idea in general

Some financial advisors will tell you to avoid credit cards no matter what. Even with the idea of having a rewards program in place, they may say that credit cards ultimately ensnare people and accrue interest. This may be true, depending on your personality. If you're someone who is able to live within your means and will always be able to pay off your credit card total each month, then you shouldn't have to worry about getting stuck in a debt trap. However, if you are someone who makes late payments and struggles to stay on top of things financially, then you should avoid credit cards. The temptation to just spend money now and pay for it later can be too great. Debt, like all things financial, should be treated with respect.

#23 Establish a Comparison Website

If you're interested in affiliate marketing and are looking for ideas of how to make a good affiliate website, then you might want to consider establishing a comparison website. A comparison website is simple to make and can be exceptionally profitable because it is specifically designed to target consumers who are looking to make purchases.

A comparison website simply compares products that are similar. A good one goes in depth, reviewing both products thoroughly and providing a point by point analysis of prices, values and features. And most importantly, you provide affiliate links so that when the purchasing decision has been made by the visitor, they can simply click on your link and buy the product, providing you with a commission.

Tips for Success

Find Niche Products

Remember that the internet is a big place and people are constantly searching for reviews and comparisons of similar products. Try to find a product section that is underserved by comparison websites. If you can find multiple types of the same products that don't have a large amount of comparison sites, you can tap into that market and collect all of that sweet traffic with the help of good SEO practices.

Be as Accurate as Possible in Research

If you want people coming back to your website, time and time again, you're going to have to establish that you are trustworthy. This requires that you be willing to be as accurate as possible in your research, spending the time and energy studying up on the various products you are covering. Learn as much as you can, and if you're really dedicated, maybe even consider purchasing the products yourself so that you can create demonstration videos. The more comprehensive your research is, the less time your viewers will have to spend looking elsewhere for more information.

Frequently Asked Questions and Answers

Q: Why wouldn't people simply look for comparisons on the product's homepage?

A: It's the same reason that most of us don't trust car salesmen: at the end of the day, they'll do just about anything to make a sale. A product website won't tell you the shortcomings of the product or admit to fault. They certainly won't show their inferiority to other products. Visiting a product comparison site is all about learning the actual truth. Are the company claims valid? Are there better products out there? Are there cheaper products out there? These are all serious questions that consumers ask when making purchasing decisions. Most companies won't answer these questions honestly.

Q: How do you make money with a comparison site?

A: You make money through affiliate links. By guiding consumers in making the right purchasing decision or by creating awareness of other competing products, you'll be able to get clicks that will translate into commissions.

Myths About Building a Comparison Website

Myth: People don't bother with much product research

This is patently false. People tend to want to hold onto their money, only parting with it when they have a significant reason to do so. Fortunately, they are often looking for reasons to spend their hard earned money. Research is one of the things that helps them get over the natural hurdles of spending money. If a customer is able to determine that they will have a good experience and that their lives will improve after purchasing the product, they will do so. And so most people spend their time researching products to determine if they are going to get the best value for their dollar. By having the ability to direct them between similar products, you are increasing their options as well as increasing the chance of getting a referral bounty from their purchase!

#24: Develop a software program

If you have the time and the skillset, then you might want to consider developing a software program, something that meets a serious market need. It doesn't always need to be a big, serious project either, sometimes the best types of programs are small but meet a niche need.

Tips for Success

Solve your own problem

If you want to make a good software program, then it'll need to solve some kind of problem for the user. The best place to find that problem is to look at your own life. What problems are you facing that could be solved by the creation of a software program? Once you are able to determine what problem you want to be solved, you can then go about creating the program.

Build hype early

Once you have a good idea and have begun working on your program, you should begin work on building hype as soon as possible. Share pictures of what you are making on social media, set up a website with a countdown. Talk about it on Reddit and other platforms. In short, do everything you can get as much hype as possible, so that when you finally do release the program, people will be excited to purchase what you've made.

Frequently Asked Questions and Answers

Q: Should I hire a team to develop an idea I have?

A: There isn't an easy answer to this question. Many times, people have great ideas on paper, but the execution can be too difficult to pull off easily. If you have the budget, time and vision to direct a creative time to develop a software program, you should make sure that you are really ready to spend a significant chunk of time managing the project.

Myth: Adding more developers means faster development time

Developing software isn't the same as building a house. Adding more developers to the stack adds more complexity, which in turn needs to be managed properly. While having multiple developers can be beneficial in a number of ways, don't just think that you can automatically increase turnaround time by hiring three more hands on deck.

#25: Rent or Lease Out Expensive Equipment

If you own equipment that isn't cheap to purchase, but don't have much use for it right now, you can make some money by leasing them out. And rather than have to deal with making these kinds of arrangements yourself and putting out ads online for people to see, you can just use one of the many different types of rental companies out there who will help you to rent out different things.

Tips for Success

Rent out your Camera Equipment

If you have access to camera equipment, then you should know that a good set up isn't cheap. Instead of just letting your cameras sit around, collecting dust when you are photographing, why not make a profit by renting out your gear? There are websites out there, such as Kitsplit, that allow for you to rent out your cameras as well as insure them, to make sure that your investment isn't damaged.

Frequently Asked Questions and Answers

Q: What else can I lend out?

A: There are no shortages of websites out there that can let you lend out your equipment to others. You can lend parking spaces, boats and even power tools. By visiting places like RentNotBuy or Loanables, you can get an idea of what else you can rent out.

#26: Purchase an established online business

If you've got the money to spend, but don't to go through all of the work of finding a niche, building a website, establishing a brand and then working to bring in traffic, you might want to consider purchasing an established online business. Doing so is fairly easy. All you need to do is a visit a website that lists online businesses for sale and browse until you find one you want. Then you just make an offer and if everything goes well, you'll have the website, the design and all the branding that has been established.

Tips for Success

Determine What You Want

Are you looking for a starter store? One that hasn't made any money but is fully built and ready to go? Or are you looking for an established business that is already making money? In the case of a starter, it'll be fairly cheap for you to acquire, but you'll need to spend quite a bit of time and money on marketing to get people visiting your product.

Buying an established business that has a monthly revenue stream is usually the best option, but it will be far more costly. You'll have to pay their asking price, which is usually multiple times their monthly revenue.

Investigate the Reason for Selling:

Some people put together businesses simply because they are interested in selling the end product. They create a well designed website, find the right niche and then tie it all together with a bow to be sold. If that's the case, then you shouldn't have to worry about the potential sales of the company. However, you may find that certain online businesses are being sold because they simply aren't making the money that they used to. The owner is either experiencing losses or just doesn't have the passion to keep the business running anymore. Either way, you'll have to deal with the fallout of a weakened brand.

Of course, most reputable exchange websites will help deal with the investigation process. Websites like Shopify's Exchange Marketplace allows for safe and effective purchases, with a higher degree of transparency.

Frequently Asked Questions and Answers

Q: What are the costs of buying an online business?

A: The cost greatly varies, but it is usually determined by the overall revenue the website brings in. High revenue websites sell for very high. Low or no revenue websites will sell for cheap.

Myths about Buying Online Businesses

Myth: If I buy an online business with a high revenue stream, I won't have to do any work!

A company has high revenue for a multitude of reasons: they have a good product, they have repeat customers, people believe in the brand, etc. However, just because an online business is currently making lots of money doesn't guarantee that it will always be that way. Businesses require maintenance. Fortunately, with the use of virtual assistants and automated social media, you should be able to keep the amount of time you spend working on the company at a minimum. But don't make the assumption that the moment you buy a high revenue company, it'll stay that way forever.

#27: Sell Online Businesses

As we mentioned in the section above, there are plenty of different places where you can buy and sell online businesses. Some people, however, have made a living off of creating Shopify businesses and other websites and then flipping them for a profit. Sometimes the profit is small, other times the profit can be great, it really depends on the niche and what future trends are pointing towards.

Creating online businesses to sell is a bit like speculation, you're looking at what is coming down the pipeline in ways of future popularity, and then making guesses as to what will be attractive as a business. If you hit the right niche, you could potentially flip your business for much more than it cost for you to make it. If you're wrong, you'll be stuck with a website that won't go anywhere.

Tips for success

Pay attention to trends

The tastes of consumers change over the years. However, we can see glimpses of the future by paying close attention to what is currently trending in popular culture. By closely following trends, you can make predictions about will grow in popularity in the future. This then translates into the ability to create websites and online businesses that anticipate the market shifts in the future.

Have strong branding

A good brand can be just as valuable as the business itself. In today's online economy, most people are looking for brands that can align with them, brands that speak to their individual form of expression. In marketing terms, branding is really just a combination of colors, logo and vision that are packaged and presented to customers. The more attractive brand that you develop, the more motivated a potential buyer will be to purchase your website from you.

Frequently Asked Questions and Answers

Q: How much does it cost to sell business websites?

A: The costs are low, but you will have to invest a certain amount of money in building the actual website itself. This means you'll have to pay for things like graphic design, logo creation, hosting fees and domain names. However, after those costs have been accounted for, you'll only need to pay the listing fees for putting your website up on an exchange.

Myth: I just need to make a great looking website and it'll sell for a lot!

While visual design is an important aspect of selling an online business, it's only a component. You'll need to have other factors that will make your business look attractive enough to potential buyers. Factors such as: revenue, strong brand identity, established fanbase, high website traffic, good product development and competitive pricing will all contribute together to help motivate an entrepreneur to purchase your product.

#28: Get into Business Franchising

If you've developed a successful business model for a company that you run, you might want to consider turning it into a franchise model. Franchises are a great way to develop passive income, as they allow for you to license out the ideas, brand packaging and techniques of your business to other people. More importantly, those people will be required to pay you a franchise fee to open up their own franchise and on top of that, will be required to pay a royalty based on their income as well. So if you have a brick and mortar type of business that is doing well, you can certainly crank up your passive income generation through starting a franchise model.

Tips for Success

Build a plan

Creating a franchise is extremely complicated and will take a lot of time. The most important part of getting started is getting everything organized and making a proper plan. You should work to create a clear idea of how you will gain franchisees, what their roles will be, what you will be providing them in terms of assistance and training and most importantly, what your fees will be. Once you have all of that put together, you should be able to continue down the road of starting a franchise.

Hire Legal Advice

An attorney will be necessary for creating the paperwork that will let you start your franchise system. You'll need to have everything ironed out so that when a franchisee agrees to take on your brand and pay you a fee, everything is above board. The last thing you want is for your franchise to hit a nasty lawsuit because you didn't properly put the paperwork together and now you're liable for a franchisee's mistakes.

Keep a tight leash on your brand

One of the most important thing about franchises is that while the owners and operators are different from the creator, the brand is still the same. This means that whatever a franchisee does, customers will associate it with any other franchise out there. This is why you'll need to keep a tight leash on your brand and ensure that your franchisees are high quality individuals who will follow the rules and represent your brand well. The last thing you want is for someone wearing your brand's uniforms and mishandling your products, which in turn creates a negative image towards all other franchises. A franchise is a great way to make money, but only if everyone is able to represent the brand properly.

This also means limiting variance within your franchise. In general, people expect the same thing from franchise to franchise. This is why, no matter which McDonald's you visit, you'll know that you can buy burgers and not spaghetti. If a franchisee begins changing how they sell your products, making additions or selling things that are not a part of your brand packaging, you can run the risk of disparity between stores. This can lead to disappointment, if say, a customer went Store A and received a product only sold in that store. They then go to Store B in another city and find out that the products were only available at Store A. This can cause confusion and in turn, weaken your brand parity.

Frequently Asked Questions and Answers

Q: How much does it cost to start franchising?

A: It depends on the size of your business, but in general, you can expect to spend a few thousand on creating training material, brand packages and meetings with potential franchisees. On top of that, you can also expect to spend quite a bit in legal fees for all the paperwork. These can range upwards to the tens of thousands. Therefore, it is safe to say that Franchising is only for a very serious entrepreneur who wants to take their already successful concept and make money with it.

Myths about Franchising

Myth: Selling a franchise can limit my own profits. Why not just open up another store?

It's easy to think that opening up a second store will be better than franchising out your business idea, but opening another store requires a significant amount of work. Moreover, it also requires a substantial investment of capital to purchase the buildings, hire the employees, train the managers, etc. Yes, you can get all of that investment back, but you're taking a risk. However, with the franchise model, you're transferring the risk to other individuals. They will have to do most of the legwork and be the ones to spend their hard earned money on location and training, all the while you get a fee and a percentage of their profits.

Besides, with a franchise system, you'll be able to ensure that your brand operates in cities where you don't live. Sure, you might be able to open a second or third location in a neighboring city, but what about halfway across the country? With franchisees opening stores on your behalf, you can still have your brand sprinkled across the country, but they're the ones who are handling the day to day operations, not you.

#29: Get into Retail Arbitrage using eBay

Retail arbitrage is the simple practice of finding products that are in demand on eBay and then finding ways to access those products below the market value. In other words, you're buying low and selling high. The trick to retail arbitrage is to learn how to do market research, to find exactly which products are in high demand. Then it's a matter of sourcing those products and then flipping them for a quick profit. This is different than simply selling on eBay, because you're actively targeting market needs, not just selling products that you collect.

Tips for Success

Use good software

If you're going to be searching for products that are in demand online, then you have two options. You can do the research by hand, which is a painstaking and miserable process, or you can use software that is designed to provide you with the most up to date information about what is selling on eBay. Software like Terapeak allows for you to quickly research what top areas arc on the eBay market, what prices are looking like and how to optimize your listings. This will help you focus on the next vital step in retail arbitrage: selling.

Move quickly

Once you've figured out which product categories are selling well, and you're able to determine what you want to sell, you'll need to move quickly. Those who are able to source the in-demand product and sell it fast enough will be the ones who reap the rewards. If you take your time, you might end up too late to the party.

Frequently Asked Questions and Answers

Q: What is the cost of retail arbitrage?

A: Retail arbitrage is one of the cheaper options when it comes to online income ideas. The only prices you have to pay are the eBay fees and the cost of acquiring goods. This means that you can scale your business as low as you like. So if you don't have a lot of money to work with, you can start out small and then work your way up, taking your investments and reinvesting it into your sales.

Myths about Retail Arbitrage

Myth: Sourcing products has gotten too difficult to do cheaply

Some of the conventional wisdom holds that finding cheap products has gotten harder and harder, thanks to the influence of people who are all focusing on the same products. However, this means that the harder it is to find products, the more they will sell for online. You'll just need to spend more time hustling to find the right products and think through less conventional channels, such as finding specific wholesalers or spending your weekends at flea markets.

#30 Start a Podcast

Podcasts are one of the most rapidly growing forms of entertainment and as such, it is becoming quite the business model. With long form audio content in such demand, podcasts are making money through hosting ads provided by sponsors. In turn, the sponsors pay based on a certain number of listens that each podcast receives. This can turn a fun, enjoyable hobby into a great way to rack up the online dollars.

Tips for Success

Focus on a good format

A good format can make or break a show. Some formats, such as one-on-one interviews or lengthy discussions about topics are reliable, but others, such as a group of friends just sitting around making jokes can be overdone. If you want to make a good podcast, then you're going to need to figure out a format that keeps people engaged and interested in what you are talking about. Do some research to determine which podcasting formats are most successful, and which ones should be avoided.

Pick a unique and interesting topic

Generalist podcasts don't work very well, unless the podcast host is already someone famous. Bill Burr's show does very well, not because of the subjects that he covers, but because people enjoy his personality, a personality this well-known from his stand-up comedy routine. So, unless you are already famous, it's best to avoid having a generalist show.

Instead, you should focus on picking a specific subject that you know well and are passionate about. Don't worry too much about picking the "right" topic as much as you should worry about picking a topic that is right for you. If you can get excited about the idea, then you should have no trouble talking about it at a length.

You should also make sure that you aren't covering a podcast topic that hasn't already been covered to death. Do some market research before you begin your podcast and make sure that your big idea doesn't already have 8,000 other podcasts covering that same subject.

Invest in a good microphone

You don't have to have incredible or expensive audio gear, but you should at least have a decent microphone, one that operates well and sounds crisp. Fortunately, with today's technology, you won't have to spend a fortune on a decent mic. You can find a great microphone, such as a Blue Yeti, for under $100, which will create great audio. You don't have to have amazing, studio grade audio quality, but you should at least invest a little so that your voice sounds crisp and clear.

Frequently Asked Questions and Answers

Q: How many listeners do I need before I can start making money?

A: It depends on the type of sponsorship you're going for, but in general, you want to get to the point where you have at least a few thousand weekly listeners. This will help make your podcast more attractive to sponsors.

Myths about Podcasting

Myth: No one cares about audio content anymore

While it may be easy to look at video content as the future, the fact remains that there are certain times that you just can't watch videos or browse on social media. As commutes are getting longer, some people are turning to podcasts as a way to enjoy the long car ride. Others tend to listen to shows while doing work that doesn't require a lot of thinking. Audio content still has a major place in our modern culture and isn't going away any time soon!

#31 Create a Latest Deals Newsletter

Another great idea to boost your affiliate marketing system would be to create a newsletter that sends people the latest deals on certain types of products. And of course, these newsletters would have affiliate links within them, ensuring that you get a nice commission anytime a reader buys a product through your letter.

To create a latest deals newsletter, you'll need to first create an email list and then a way for people to find it. You'll most likely want to host the email list opt-in on your website, so that people who visit your site will be able to sign up for the newsletter.

Tips for Success

Offer attractive deals

The deals that you offer should be attractive. You might be able to work with your affiliate publisher to get access to exclusive deals that you can then send through these newsletters. This would be a great way to motivate people to be willing to sign up for your service. Most importantly, if you are offering attractive deals with significant savings, you will increase the chances of generating sales for yourself.

Don't bombard subscribers

When people have signed up for your newsletter, they are trusting that you will treat them kindly and respectfully. As a sign of respect, you should refrain from heavily bombing them with newsletters each and every day. Instead, focus on sending a few, high quality letters a week, making sure not to inundate your subscribers with too much stuff. Too many emails and they could end up unsubscribing, frustrated with your newsletter. If that's the case, they might transfer that frustration to your website as well and stop visiting!

Frequently Asked Questions and Answers

Q: What's the best way to gain subscribers to my newsletter?

A: The most tried and true method would be by creating a free gift or a special offer that only subscribers get access to. This will generate more subscribers due to interest in obtaining the free gift.

Myths about Newsletters

Myth: Most newsletters go straight to the trash

While this may be true in some cases, the good news is that with newsletters we have access to analytics. With the power of analytics we can determine how many people open up and read the emails that we send out. This gives us the ability to see how effective our newsletters are. If the majority of people are simply deleting and not reading them, we can make modifications to improve our email, either by changing the frequency of our emails or by changing the quality of the deals. You'll find that even though there are people who will just delete newsletters, thanks to analytics, you can monitor these people and just remove them from your list.

#32 Create WordPress Themes

If you have a knack for good website design, you might want to consider creating and selling premium WordPress Themes. People are always looking for enjoyable and eye-catching themes for their websites, browsing through both blogs and the WordPress Theme Catalog looking for opportunities to find the best themes.

Tips for Success

Find a Marketplace

With WordPress being one of the most popular content management systems out there, you don't need to look very far to find a place to sell your theme. Marketplaces like Themeforest or Mojo, you'll be able to list your Theme and sell it for the price that you want.

Take Custom Orders

Some people have great ideas for web design, but don't have a clue on how to make the website themselves. You should work to position yourself so that people are aware that you can take custom orders for WordPress themes. This will give you a much higher income potential than just selling Themes to anyone online, as custom web design often costs much more.

Frequently Asked Questions and Answers

Q: What do people look for in a WordPress theme?

A: While there are plenty of free themes out there to choose from, most people who buy premium themes are looking for a higher level of functionality. Advanced features, drag and drop and the ability to customize basic things like banners quickly are all attractive to buyers. If you want to make your theme different from the rest, don't just focus on making the theme beautiful, also work to give it unique features that other Themes don't have.

119

#33: Invest in Dividend Stocks

A great way to turn your savings into quarterly payouts is by investing in dividend stocks. Some publicly traded stock companies wish to offer an incentive to keep investors holding onto their stock. This incentive is usually a percentage of the profit, paid out to all shareholders. These payouts are known as dividends. The best part is that you don't have to do anything special in order to obtain these dividend sharing stocks, all you need to do is buy them. Then, you'll get an annual payout based on the profits of that company!

Tips for Success

Look for proven companies

Larger, established companies with longstanding histories should be your primary target when looking for good stocks to choose from. These companies won't suffer from too much volatility, and most importantly, will be able to afford to pay out a dividend each year.

Diversify

One of the most basic principles of investment is diversification. No matter what approach you want to take towards getting dividends, whether aggressive or conservative, you should spread out your investments across a few different stocks in different sectors. This will protect you from any sharp changes in the market or unexpected downturns.

Frequently Answered Questions and Answers

Q: How much can I make off of dividend stocks?

A: The payouts are determined by two things, the percentage of profit the company is willing to share and the amount of shares that you own. If they offer a 3% yield, and you've invested 1,000, you're looking at earning $30 a year. So, that number isn't terribly exciting for passive income. You'll find that if you want to really make a lot of money with dividends, you'll need to have invested quite a bit to get there. However, that money is usually better off sitting in a dividend than it is in a bank account.

Myths about Dividend Stocks

Myth: Dividend Stocks do well no matter what

While it might seem like everyone would keep their money in a dividend stock, which in turn keeps the price of the stock healthy, the fact is that people are emotional creatures. When markets begin to take a downturn, when bad news comes out or when a company misses earnings, there are a wide number of people who will see this as a catastrophe, trigging them to sell. This sudden run could cause just about any stock to drop in value. The good news is that unless the dividend stock company is looking to get rid of even more people, they will most likely continue offering the dividend. If that's the case, then you might want to simply just buy more at the lower price. However, it is also possible that the company could stop offering the dividend in the hopes of gathering more capital for themselves. If that's the case, you can expect to see the stock price drop quickly.

#34: Establish an Authority Site

An authority site is just that, a website that has the authority to speak definitively on certain matters.

These sites are trusted sources of information and people flock to these sites knowing that they can trust what has been written about the subject. Usually, authority sites are similar to blogs in the sense that they share a significant amount of content. However, unlike a blog, they are highly targeted to a single niche. The goal of an authority site is to become an authority on one and only one niche. This translates to a higher level of concentrated traffic, which is then monetized through the use of affiliate marketing.

Tips for Success

Focus on High Quality

Authority sites are different from blogs because they focus on developing not only high quality material, but also high quality web design. You simply must have a sharp looking website that is fast, responsive and sleek. People should have no trouble searching for topics and they shouldn't be plagued by annoying things, such as unsightly pop-ups bugging them every few seconds. The higher the quality that your website is, the more people will automatically assume that you are an authority on the subject matter.

Pick a niche

You must pick a niche and then focus only on creating content in that niche. You should not waste your time or energy writing about anything else. An authority site is not a blog, it's not a place for personal asides and long rants. While those things are fine for a simple blog model, an authority site is hyper focused on a single topic. This will drive in much more traffic of like-minded people who, if your content is good, will eventually end up visiting your website whenever they want more information about the niche you've chosen.

Frequently Asked Questions and Answers

Q: What are the costs of making an authority site?

A: While you will have to incur the regular costs of domain name and web hosting, you'll most likely want to spend some money on web design as well. Getting a good looking and extremely responsive website design isn't the most expensive thing in the world, but it does cost a bit of money. However, what really differentiates an authority site from a blog is presentation. You should be willing to spend a bit of extra money in order to make your authority site look like it has authority, just from a glance!

Myths about Authority Sites

Myth: Authority Sites are identical to blogs

While at a first glance, authority sites may seem to be identical to blogs, it is important to remember that a blog serves multiple purposes. A blog is a place to share your voice, connect with others, talk about any topic that interests you and generally link people to stuff you care about, such as your own products. The biggest topic in a blog is really you, as you are free to share as much info about your personal journey as you like.

Authority sites are laser focused, narrowly aiming at only a niche market and then staying as focused on that content as possible. Authority sites don't waver and don't move away from their target market, ever. They are also hyper-monetized as well, focusing on generating traffic so that they are able to sell their affiliate links to the right kind of people. The two websites might seem similar at first, but in truth they are worlds apart.

#35: Create a membership site

Membership sites are similar to blogs, except that they require a premium membership in order to access the premium articles. This is a great way to turn an already popular blog into passive income, as it allows for you to entice your current readers into paying for membership access to the good parts of your blog.

Tips for Success

Use a premium plugin

Setting up a membership site isn't difficult. All you need to do is find a premium membership plugin on WordPress and you'll have everything you need to set up a gateway that allows only people with paid memberships to access specific content on your blog.

Entice with Previews

Some plugins allow for you to create preview pages, where the top of the article can be read for free, but in order to access the rest of the content, you'll need to pay to be a member. Make sure that you use the best, most enticing content to convince people that the product you are offering is worth spending the money!

Frequently Asked Questions and Answers

Q: Will people be upset if I use a paywall?

: It depends on how you integrate it. If you take content that was already free and put it behind a paywall, you will undoubtedly anger your fans and will most likely take a severe hit in traffic. However, if you are willing to communicate these changes ahead of time, offer free months for those who are already following you and only put new, specific types of content behind the paywall, you should be fine.

Myths about Membership Sites

Myth: People won't pay for content

If you have good and interesting content, stuff that is attractive and that answers problems, you won't have to worry about motivating people to pay for content. If there is a market need, there will be people who are willing to make the purchase. All you need to focus on is creating attractive advertisements on your website, so that people will see the benefit of the product and purchase it accordingly.

#36 Use a High-Yield Savings Account

Traditional savings account are fairly terrible when it comes to annual yield. The percentages are tightly regulated and can't even shelter your money from the annual inflation rates. Instead of letting your savings just sit around, collecting a nickel's worth of interest each year, you should look to using a high-yield savings account instead.

Tips for Success

Use a money market account

Money market accounts are great ways to save your money, while enjoying a competitive yield that is much higher than your regular savings account. When you put your money in a money market account, the bank will then begin to invest that money, but targeting only safe investments. They will then share with you a higher yield rate, since they are using their money for investing. The good news is that your account is still FDIC insured, so you aren't risking anything by giving them your money.

Frequently Asked Questions and Answers

Q: Can I get my money out of money market accounts when I want?

A: Most money market accounts do work slower than regular banks when it comes to getting your money out of them. However, you can find money market accounts that offer check writing privileges, so that you don't have to worry about suddenly being stuck in an emergency and having no money to handle it.

Myths about High-Yield Savings Account

Myth: The rates on High-Yield Accounts aren't still that high, so why bother?

You might not be terribly excited about a 2-2.5% annual yield, however, you should realize that that the higher your savings account yield is, the more you are going to be able to protect your money from inflation. Inflation happens on a yearly basis. An inflation rate of a mere 1.5 percent could cause the money sitting in a regular savings account to lose value. You don't want your hard earned money to lose value, so it's important that you find ways to protect it from minimal levels of inflation!

#37: Rent Out Your Vehicles

If you have a car but you aren't using it much, then you might want to consider renting it out! It works the same as most other rental systems, you simply use an app or company to facilitate the rental. Then the customer makes the purchase, gets the keys and goes about their business. Then, the car is brought back (gassed up, mind you) and you get paid!

Rent out your Car with Turo

Turo allows for users to rent out their cars to people by listing them on their website. Then, customers can pay a fee, rent the vehicle for x amount of days and both Turo and you get paid. Best of all, Turo pays with direct deposit within five days of the rental. Best of all, Turo insures your vehicle so you don't have to worry about it being destroyed by a reckless driver!

#38: Rent Out Your Clothes

Clothes are an important part of society, to say the least! However, if your closets are overstuffed, full of clothes that are in good condition but nevertheless go unused, you might want to consider renting them out to make some extra cash. While it might sound a little crazy, it's possible to rent out clothes by using specialty websites that facilitate such a transaction. So, if you have a closet full of gorgeous but woefully underutilized clothes, consider renting them out!

Tips for Success

Use Lending Sites

Websites such as Stylelend exist as a way for you to list your clothes online. You'll send in your clothing for inspection and they will be added to the stock. Once your clothing item has been rented by someone, you get a percentage of the rental profit!

Frequently Asked Questions and Answers

Q: Is there really a market demand for renting clothes?

A: As surprising as it is, yes there is! The cost of renting clothing vs buying is significantly cheaper. Most people want to keep their wardrobes fresh and flexible. The idea of simply renting out clothes to wear for a short time and then returning them, only to rent more clothes can be appealing to those who have rapidly changing senses of fashion. And, with today's online economy, people can get exactly what they're looking for.

#39: Rent Out Your Bikes

If you live in an area where people love to bike, then you might want to consider renting out your own bikes for people to use. It's a great way to make some money!

Tips for Success

Use a bikeshare app

There are plenty of apps that help connect people looking for a bicycle to rent to owners who are willing to part with their bicycle for a day. By listing your bike or other sports gear on these websites, you'll be able to raise earn money, just for letting strangers use your gear!

#40: Rent Out Your Garage Space/Parking Space

In some cities, parking can be extremely expensive and hard to come by! If you find that you have access to a parking space, or garage spaces where people can park, you might want to consider renting it out to people for a discounted rate. This can be a great way to monetize space that you otherwise aren't using.

Use a peer-to-peer space app

Websites like Parklee or Pavermint give people the ability to find parking spaces that are being offered by individuals. There, they can find the parking spot they're looking for and then rent it out. All you have to do is make sure that the space is empty and you can collect your fee! This can be great if you're on vacation, or own property in a busy city that has very expensive parking.

#41: Rent out storage space

If you're looking at an empty garage, or a big shed without anything inside of it, you could turn that empty space into dollar bills by renting out the storage capacity! It's no secret that monthly storage can be quite expensive, and people might not want to spend a fortune on storing only a few small ticket items. If that's the case, they might be interested in using someone else's space as a storage solution, in exchange for a cheaper price tag!

Tips for Success

Use a peer-to-peer storage website

Websites like storeatmyhouse.com allow for you to list your free space online. This listing will allow for you to rent out the space without having to interact directly with the client.

Keep the storage area clear of your own stuff

If you're going to be renting out a storage area, then it is important that you ensure that your stuff can't be readily accessed. This is so that you don't have to worry about items going missing. This allows for the client to be able to access only their items, without fear of you going in and out of their stuff constantly either.

#42: Earn Money and Rewards Watching Videos and TV

If you like to watch videos and television, but lament the fact that you aren't making any money from it, don't worry! There are ways for you to turn your favorite hobby into a cash making machine!

Tips for Success

Take Surveys after Watching Videos

You can get paid by companies like inbox dollars, who will pay you a rate after you take a survey on a video or trailer that you have watched on their behalf. This is how companies are able to get important data about how audiences feel about certain movies, marketing efforts, etc.

Become a Certified Field Associate

A certified field associate, working for Marketforce information, is someone who goes to movie theaters and performs tasks such as "theater checks" to determine how many patrons are in a film. You can get paid for performing these activities and on top of that, you'll also be able to get compensation for the films that you go to watch. So if you're constantly going to the theater, then you might want to consider a side-gig of being a CFA.

Frequently Asked Questions and Answers

Q: Are taking surveys really a good way to get paid?

A: It really depends on the survey company. Some companies offer mediocre rewards and require a significant amount of surveys to be offered before you get anything close to a decent payout. Others are more generous, but also have more serious requirements. It really depends on how hard you are willing to look and how hard you are willing to work.

Myths about Making Money Watching Videos

Myth: All survey companies are scam artists

While it is true that there are survey companies that use false pretenses as a way to get people to fill out their surveys, not all of them are scam artists. Data is one of the most vital things to entertainment companies, and surveys are a great way to collect that data. If you are considering using a survey company, you should spend a considerable amount of time doing the proper research to see if they are right for you.

#43: Launch a Vending Machine Business

Vending machines are a tried and true method of generating passive income. All you need is good real estate, a great vending machine and a consistent stock schedule to ensure that people have constant access to your goods.

Tips for Success

Location is Everything

Finding an ideal location for your vending machine is one of the most important parts of the entire business model. A high-traffic area, preferably without other food competition is ideal. Of course, acquiring the rights to that location can be troublesome. You'll need to negotiate with the owner of the property, offer them a percentage of the profits or outright be required to pay rent for the space itself.

But if you get a high traffic area, you can make quite a bit of money!

Stock only winners

There are some tried and true products that will sell in a vending machine. Instead of getting weird and experimental, hoping to catch some niche market, you've got to remember that the general public will be interacting with your machine. So, stick to what is proven to work. Sell candies, snacks and sodas, with a few healthier options for those who are health conscious.

Frequently Asked Questions and Answers

Q: How much does it cost to run a vending machine?

A: In general, you'll want to acquire a good machine that accepts both cash and credit cards. Depending on your budget and the model of machine you acquire, you can start for as low as $1,000.

Myths about Vending Machines

Myth: Running a vending machine operation takes little effort

This is false! Once the vending machine operation has taken off, you will find that you won't have to expend as much energy to keep things moving, but before that, you should be prepared to put in quite a bit of time in creating a business plan, scouting locations and finding the right place for your machine.

#44: Create music and license it out

If you're musically talented and enjoy making music, but don't want to compete in the professional music world, there are other options to make money. One of the easiest ways is to create music specifically tailored for certain types of videos or presentations and then sell a generic use license.

Tips for Success

Create music for markets

When creating music as art, you'll want to focus on individual expression and personal taste. However, when making music to license out, you should change your focus. Instead of making what you like, try to identify market needs and create music that caters to those needs. For example, as podcasting grows, the demand for simple, cheap intro music has grown. Look for niches and create music in those areas.

Create Royalty Free Music

When a company is looking for music to purchase, most of the time they don't want to deal with any strings attached. This means rather than simply license out music, they'd rather just pay the larger fee and get a royalty free version.

Frequently Asked Questions and Answers

Q: Where can I sell my music?

A: You can sell your music either on your own websites, or you can place them in online markets that sell stock music. You'll make more money selling on your own website and you'll be able to establish a brand, but then you'll have to put money and time into marketing.

#45: Earn money on cashback sites

If you enjoy shopping online, you might want to consider using a cashback website. Cashback websites offer rebates through online programs, providing you with money or gift cards whenever you purchase items through their affiliate stores. This is a good way to get some of your money back after spending it on the things that you were going to buy anyway!

Tips for Success

Look for the best offers

There are plenty of cashback websites out there to choose from. Instead of just signing up for the first one, take some time to evaluate and determine which one that works best for you. Remember, these are affiliate links that you're buying from, so make sure that you are following a cashback site that offers stuff that you're actually looking for.

#46: Look into Refinancing Your Mortgage

While it technically isn't generating any income, it is saving you money. Your financial situations do change over time and if you've found yourself to have a stronger income rate and a higher level of credit, you might want to consider refinancing. This will let you get a better interest rate, which in turn will save you money.

Tips for Success

Become as educated as possible:

Spend as much time as you can learning how refinancing works. You can certainly save money, but only if you do things right. It can be a little overwhelming with the different options and rules out there regarding refinancing. Furthermore, there can be major pitfalls if you don't do it properly. The best way to remedy these problems is to become educated. Take a few hours to study this process seriously before you even begin to consider whether or not refinancing is for you.

Frequently Asked Questions and Answers

Q: Are there costs to refinance a mortgage?

A: Yes. You will have to pay the closing costs after you've refinanced it, just as you had to pay closing costs the first time. There are also all the other usual costs associated with the loan application, such as document fees, house appraisal, etc.

Myths about Refinancing

Myth: Refinancing companies can help me!

Be very careful when it comes to working with companies that offer aid with refinancing. There can be a lot of fraudsters in this field, or people looking to take advantage of those who are in need. Take it slow, evaluate every option and make sure that you do your due diligence to determine the validity of these companies claims before you use them.

#47 Start a Patreon for Donations

If you find that the content you provide has quite a bit of fans, you might want to consider creating a Patreon. Patreon is a donation system where fans can support you by paying a monthly fee. In exchange for this support, you offer them goodies and rewards that often don't have a high monetary value but are valuable for branding reasons.

Tips for Success

Offer Tiers:

Most good patreons offer several different tiers of support. Starting the first tier off at a single dollar will enable people to just support you out of the kindness of their hearts. Offering higher tier supports, ranging from 3-10 dollars is also important. By keeping only a single tier, you are denying yourself either a higher level of profit, or are causing others to shy away because they cannot or will not meet that price point.

Offer attractive goods

A successful patreon makes their money by offering good quality content and goods that aren't accessible anywhere else. The exclusivity is what makes patreon so appealing to most users. Sure, they get the ability to support their favorite content creators, but it's the allure of the rewards that convinces them to make the first payment to begin with.

Frequently Asked Questions and Answers

Q: Is there a cost to start a patreon?

A: No, starting a patreon is free. However, Patreon does take a percentage of your monthly payouts. This is payment for the services that they offer, such as analytics, handling payments and charging patrons each month.

#48: Create an audiobook

If you've written a book and are selling it online, you might want to consider creating an audiobook version of it. Doing so isn't too hard, all you'll need is a microphone, a quiet room and the time to narrate the book.

Tips for Success

Use ACX

Audible, which is owned by Amazon, will host your audiobook as well as give you the tools you need to create a good audio experience. You can upload the finished product and then link the product to your Amazon account. After that, when people go to visit your book online, they'll see a link where they can purchase the audio version of it on Audible.

Frequently Asked Questions and Answers

Q: Should I only use Audible for selling audiobooks?

A: In short, yes! Audible is the number one seller of audiobooks, no other market comes even close. With the power of Amazon backing them, they account for the highest percentage of audiobook sales online. Audible does require that you exclusively use them, but you aren't losing out on any other market by using them. Instead, you are opening up yourself up to incredibly synergy. Audible even has what's known a whispersync technology, where a reader who owns both the audiobook and the ebook can switch between the two on the fly and still keep the same spot in the book!

Myths about creating audiobooks

Myth: My own voice sounds horrible! No one will like my book!

Everyone is shocked and most likely repelled by the sound of their own voice. Why is that? Simply because the voice we project isn't the same that we hear. The bones in our head vibrate as we speak, in turn creating a different sound. When you hear a digital capture of your own voice, you don't have the same vibration, which in turn makes your voice sound different and shocking. Don't worry, your voice is perfectly fine. If people can stand to be around when you talk, you have nothing to fear when making your own audiobook.

#49: Round up purchases with Acorns

Acorns is an app that rounds up your card purchases. For example, if you were to buy a donut that cost 1.55, Acorn would round the charge up to $2.00 even. Then, with that extra .45 cents, Acorn would invest that money into a stock, providing you with a small gain. Over time, the more that you spend of your own money, the more investing Acorn does. If you find yourself undisciplined with your investing, or you're constantly neglecting to put money aside to invest, you should consider using Acorns.

#50: Use commission free trading

If you're an investor, the last thing you want to deal with is commissions eating up your profits. Not everyone can trade in large enough volumes to make money, in fact, those who are starting out small tend to only be able to trade in small volumes. This means that each transaction can take a major hit in your bottom line. Even a ten dollar trading fee means that you're spending $20 on each buy and sell order. For short term trading, this can be extremely painful.

Fortunately, there has been a rise in commission free platforms and apps, such as Robinhood. Robinhood has a lot of the same functionality as a traditional broker, but with limited types of trades that can be done. However, by keeping things bare bones and streamlined, you won't have to worry about paying fat commissions each time you make a small trade.

Conclusion

Making passive income is possible! It takes a lot of hard work, education and the willingness to put in the hours, but if you want to make money while you sleep, you can do it! We hope that this list of 50 ways to earn passive income has given you ideas of how you can make as much money as possible!

How to Build an Online Empire from Scratch

Before we begin I have a free gift for you from Russell Brunson - for those of you that don't know Russell Brunson is, he's the man that created Click Funnels. In my opinion it's the best funnel website out there and it has also helped create the most millionaires. Any form of passive income you are going to build you will 100% need to leverage funnels of some sort. If you're reading this book, then you want to be the best in your industry. This book will give you the play by play to have people PAYING you for your advice. I am able to give you his best selling book for free right down here. I only have a few copies left so please get them while you can. Just click this http://bit.ly/giftfunnelbook

CPSIA information can be obtained
at www.ICGtesting.com
Printed in the USA
BVHW070831221119
564515BV00005B/427/P

9 781087 819143